First Edition

Author Mark Neilson
Publisher Gralison Publishing

Publisher's Note
Every possible effort has been made to ensure the accuracy of the information contained in this book at the time of going to press. The author cannot accept responsibility for any errors or omissions, however caused. No responsibility for loss or damage occasioned to any person acting, or resulting from action, as a result of the material contained in this publication can be accepted by the editor, the publisher or the author.

AuthorHouse™ UK Ltd.
500 Avebury Boulevard
Central Milton Keynes, MK9 2BE
www.authorhouse.co.uk
Phone: 08001974150

First published by AuthorHouse 5/10/2010

ISBN: 978-1-4490-7717-4 (sc)

This book is printed on acid-free paper.

Contents

Introduction

Let's not kid ourselves, it's a tough climate out there if you are looking for a job at the moment. However, it is not all 'doom and gloom', in February 2009 a quarter of a million people have found jobs. Unemployment rose as there were more people put out of work than found work but it shows there are still jobs out there! In February 2009 there were officially 445,000 jobs available through the various mediums and unbelievably, certain sectors are still experiencing skill shortages.

This book will help you identify what assistance is available to make sure you are financially able to keep looking for work and hopefully keep the bills paid. It will also help you identify the skills you have, both mentally and practically, and let you decide if training and upskilling is an option that suits you.

Most of the information included in this book is available in the public domain but **Get a Job ...Fast!** is a single point of reference bringing it all together for you.

Get a Job ...Fast! will give you the skills you need to find out where to look, what kind of job to go for, how to prepare the applications, prepare for the interviews and what to say when you get there.

Finally, it will help ensure that when you have the opportunity you....**GET A JOB ...FAST!**

Chapter One:
Let's Get Started

First things first, you may be one of the thousands who have recently lost their job - or are about to. If you are prepared to go on an aggressive job-search and 'Get that Job' you need to ensure you have the basics covered first.....and that is to ensure you have some stability behind you to enable you to spend enough time and be in the right frame of mind when you attend those interviews.

Redundancy

This can be a very stressful and worrying time and you need to know what to expect from your employer and what benefits you are able to claim.

The Department for Business, Enterprise and Regulatory Reform (BERR) can provide information and links to other websites that can assist you.

Useful Websites

www.berr.gov.uk and go to the Employment Matters page.
www.direct.gov.uk and enter redundancy into the search option.

These sites can provide plenty of information on your redundancy entitlement statutory rights and also includes a 'ready reckoner calculator' to calculate your redundancy payout.

There are very strict time limits on claiming (or disputing) redundancy pay, so ensure you find out about your rights and entitlements straight away.

Benefits

There are numerous government schemes to help people who have lost their job and you need to ensure you get the correct advice to claim your entitlements.

Jobseeker's Allowance and Income Support are the two most common benefits available.

More information is available from Job Centre Plus, which has teams of qualified and experienced advisors on hand to assist with your claim.

Useful Websites

www.jobcentreplus.gov.uk will give you more information on the types of claims available.

Additional assistance is also provided by the 'Travel-to-Interview Scheme', 'Job Grant' and 'In Work Credit'.

Jobcentre Plus can help you pay to get to your job interview, pay you a tax-free lump sum when you start work and provide a tax-free payment for parents bringing up children alone.

www.dwp.gov.uk/eservice will enable you to claim online once you know what you are entitled to.

Useful Contact Numbers

Jobcentre Plus	Tel:	0800 055 66 88
	Textphone:	0800 023 48 88

Certain benefits are available for people on low incomes or those who are having difficulty paying their mortgage or rent.

The websites above can provide more information along with:

www.direct.gov.uk which will help with Housing Benefit, the Mortgage Rescue Scheme if you are having difficulty paying your mortgage. Also on the site are details of Council Tax Benefit amongst other useful resources.

This site also includes details of the Job Grant that applies when you return to work.

Debt Advice

There are numerous places to seek help and the sooner you act the better. The government has various departments that are there to assist you with any problems you may have. www.direct.gov.uk has useful sections with contact numbers and links.

National Debtline offers free, confidential and independent help over the phone for people in England, Scotland and Wales. You can call their helpline and also download publications from their website.

www.nationaldebtline.co.uk   Tel: 0808 808 4000

Consumer Credit Counselling Service (CCCS) has a helpline providing free, independent and impartial advice to people who have debt problems.

www.cccs.co.uk   Tel: 0800 138 1111

Community Legal Advice (CLA) If you qualify for legal aid, CLA can provide free help or legal advice over the phone for problems with debt, housing, employment, education and welfare benefits and tax credits.

www.communitylegaladvice.org.uk   Tel: 0845 345 4 345

Citizens Advice Bureau (CAB) Your local CAB is a good place to find free advice. They provide free information and advice on legal, money and other problems. You can find your local CAB in the phone book or on their website.

www.citizensadvice.org.uk

Chapter Two:

Now Get Yourself Prepared

You need to take a realistic look at yourself, your work and life experience and be prepared to sell yourself positively. Break down all of your jobs, listing the skills you learned, skills you used and skills you were trained on. This will ensure that when you apply, you can emphasise your abilities that are relevant to the job and make your CV stand out.

You also need to know what you want. There is no point applying for jobs, receiving offers and then turning them down as unsuitable. This only wastes time for you and the employer.

You may be in an industry which is facing an acute downturn and you will be merely 'banging your head against a brick wall' by only applying for jobs in these sectors.

Do you need to train and how?

Taking into account your skills and experience, what you want and your previous industry, training may be an ideal option for you.

Useful Websites

www.worktrain.gov.uk is a free national online jobs and learning site provided by the Department for Work and Pensions. It provides up-to-date information on training opportunities amongst other things.

www.learndirect.co.uk offers courses at a variety of levels in a wide range of different subjects. Courses start from £19.99 but depending on your circumstances you may be eligible for funding, and if so may pay a fraction of the full cost, or nothing at all.

Self-employment

You may consider that now, possibly with a redundancy package, is the ideal time to take the decision to start your own business.

The success of any new business will partly depend on your attitude and skills. This means being honest about - your knowledge, your financial status and the personal qualities that you can bring to your new business

Useful Websites

www.businesslink.gov.uk is a free business advice and support service, available online and through local advisers

www.hmrc.gov.uk/startingup aim to help you understand some of the many things you need to think about when you're running a business, especially the main Tax and National Insurance issues.

Most of the main banks have sections on their own websites giving advice on starting a business.

It is also beneficial to get some professional advice from a solicitor and/or accountant in your area (most offer a FREE first meeting). The larger firms can usually recommend other useful contacts and can assist with cashflow forecasts etc.

Internet/PC Access

In this modern age you will certainly need use of a PC and have internet access. You will need to have an electronic copy of your CV as it is far more common to apply online for specific jobs but more importantly is the wealth of information available via the internet.

There are 3,500 public libraries in England and all local authorities have received government funding to provide free PC and internet access. Most authorities also provide access to a range of online reference materials. The number below will help you find your local library:

People's Network   Tel: 0121 345 7303

Useful Websites

www.peoplesnetwork.gov.uk has a search function to find your local library.

www.hotspot-locations.com is a directory that has a useful search facility for finding both FREE to use and pay Wi-Fi access if you already have a laptop or handheld device.

Chapter Three:
Do Your Research

This is one of the most important chapters, you have to find the job opportunities before you can apply for them. There are masses of newspapers, publications, and websites available listing literally thousands of vacancies, both temporary and permanent.

According to the ONS (Office of National Statistics), there were 504,000 job vacancies in the three months to January 2009 and you only want one of them!

Newspapers & Publications

Local Newspapers

www.newspapersoc.org.uk The newspaper society has a search facility to find all local newspapers and magazines and most are online now and include plenty of locally advertised jobs.

National Newspapers

All of the main UK national press advertise new jobs on at least one day of the week. Below you will find the full list. As you'll see many of the newspapers specialise in certain areas. Use this list to identify your chosen career so you know which papers will be the best to buy.

Financial Times - www.ft.com

Monday	Finance – Up to £40k
Wednesday	General and IT over £100k
Thursday	All other financial, Legal and IT Over £100k
Saturday	General and IT

Guardian/Observer - www.jobsunlimited.co.uk

Monday	Creative, Media, Sales & Marketing, PR, New Media and Secretarial
Tuesday	Education – Senior Appointments in Higher Education, General Appointments within Colleges & Schools
Wednesday	Executive Senior, Management, Public Sector, Social Care, Health, Housing, Regeneration, Charities and Environmental
Thursday	IT, Science, Technology and Telecommunications
Saturday	Repeat of Monday and Thursday's appointments
Sunday Observer	– repeats of Senior, IT & Telecommunications. Plus selected ads from the Guardian

Independent/Independent on Sunday - www.independent.co.uk

Monday	IT, Science, Technology and Engineering
Wednesday	Professional
Thursday	General, Public Sector, Graduate and Media
Sunday	General Appointments

Daily Telegraph/Sunday Telegraph - www.telegraph.co.uk

Thursday	General Appointments – special supplement
Sunday	Repeat from Thursday

The Times - www.the-times.co.uk
Sunday Times - www.sunday-times.co.uk

Monday	Interface & IT
Tuesday	Legal
Wednesday	Crème de la Crème Secretarial and Admin
Thursday	Crème de la Crème, Graduate, Management Plus and Premier, General Appointments and repeats from Sunday
Friday	Crème de la Crème and Media
Sunday	Executive, Public, General and Education

Daily Mail/Mail on Sunday - www.dailymail.co.uk

Friday	General Appointments
Sunday	General Appointments

Trade Journals

www.grocerjobs.co.uk has jobs from the last two issues of "The Grocer" featuring a wide selection of roles within the FMCG sector across the UK.

www.londoncareers.net list vacancies from the free magazines distributed weekly – Girl About Town, Ms London, Nine to Five and Midweek. Concentrates on the recruitment market for office jobs - secretarial, junior finance and administrative roles. Search by publication and you can view a list of direct or agency jobs.

www.newscientistjobs.com allows you to search their database for hundreds of science jobs. Registration is free and you can upload your CV, set up email job alerts, subscribe to RSS feeds and apply for science jobs online.

Job-Boards/Sites

Job Boards and Job Sites are dedicated to helping you find your next job. Most are not recruitment agencies, but lots of agencies and employers use their websites every day.

They are mostly free to use and link to various websites that advertise jobs paid for by the employers themselves.

www.broadbean.com/job-boards lists all of major boards in the UK and hundreds of other specialist and niche job boards. The network reaches and also supports job boards in Europe, US, Asia and Australia and is currently the fastest growing job board network in the world.

www.jobcentreplus.gov.uk has around one third of all jobs advertised in the UK.

www.twitterjobsearch.com the new blogging phenomenon, now has a job search facility with over 30,000 jobs added per week.

www.1job.co.uk has 300,000+ jobs from employment agencies and employers.

The six sites below are owned by Trinity Mirror plc and have over 3.7 million registered candidates across its portfolio of job sites. They receive over 1.8 million visits, 3.3 million searches and 446,000 applications per month.

www.jobsearch.co.uk
www.secsinthecity.co.uk
www.totallylegal.com
www.planetrecruit.com
www.thecareerengineer.com
www.gaapweb.com

www.jobsin.co.uk links to individual websites for each job sector. A wide range of job areas including more unusual sector breakdowns such as: airport, care support, forestry, prisons and veterinary. Good geographical searching as you can search within a certain radius of a town or city.

www.jobsite.co.uk has a number of recruiters who submit jobs to this site. An A-Z list is provided with the number of vacancies each recruiter has live. There are around 15,000 live vacancies at any one time and the site handles over 60,000 jobs a month. Particularly strong on middle management positions which can be searched by keyword, date, permanent or contract, location, skills, job title and sector.

www.monster.co.uk is the largest and longest established job bank. Provide options to search by region, industry/function, full-time/part-time, temporary or contract work together with keyword searching. There is also a separate search page for Scotland or you can expand your search to Europe or other countries/continents.

www.reed.co.uk is the UK's largest job site with over 100,000 jobs across all sectors. There are only a small % of jobs actually being handled by Reed's office network as the site offers advertising for companies recruiting directly too.

www.topjobs.co.uk started in 1996, this is one of the longest established UK job boards. TopJobs offers a wide selection of middle management and senior roles. Select the country you wish to search and select jobs by country, main functional area with option for sub-sector, region, date range and keyword.

www.totaljobs.co.uk is a job bank from Reed Business Information. It had broad coverage and friendly search facility with a database of approximately 30,000 jobs.

Direct to Employers

Around 30% of all jobs aren't advertised externally at all. If you know which organisation you want to work for, check their recruitment pages regularly and sign up for any news alerts on offer. Also, check online for the business listings that will provide contact details in your area.

If your details land on a decision maker's desk, even if they don't have a position now, they may contact you rather than advertise when one arises.

This is a more proactive way to approach your job search and is an excellent way of indicating your availability and getting your name out into the market place. Identify a list of companies that you would be keen to work for and who would be interested in what you have to offer. Having made this list, you need to call each one and get the correct name of the HR Manager or person dealing with recruitment, as it is crucial that your letter and CV land on the desk of the appropriate decision maker.
Use your professional trade organisation, they are a great resource for job leads, mentoring and research. Professional associations can also keep you 'in the loop'. Contact other professionals to tell them of your goals and to ask for guidance. You never know when one might say "Call this person and say I referred you."

Job Fairs

A great opportunity to find numerous employers with jobs all in one place. You will need to have plenty of hard copy CV's to take with you. Dress as if you are attending an interview and treat your conversation with the representative as if you are applying for the job – remember first impressions.

Most local job fairs are organised by your local paper, call them or check their website for upcoming events.

Networking

Networking is the process of interacting with others to exchange information and experiences for mutual benefit. We all network in our personal and professional lives, for all sorts of reasons - e.g. meeting new people at a party, discovering that a friend of a friend has interests in common with you.

Developing a network of contacts can help you research your career ideas, and could also get you a job. Even if you have never networked before it doesn't mean you don't already have the contacts.

Old school, college or university classmates
Family members
Neighbours
Your friends/partners families
Your doctor, solicitor or accountant
Former colleagues or bosses
Club members or anyone else you meet socially
Review your whole email address book

The Internet has made networking a viable option for everyone and there are many forums and business networking sites which enable business people to share and discuss their views and knowledge.

Useful Websites

www.en.wikipedia.org/wiki will list all of the main social networking sites when entered into the search engine.

www.friendsreunited.co.uk is useful for finding old school friends and work colleagues.

www.facebook.com is the UK's leading social networking site.

www.linkedin.com is an interconnected network of experienced professionals from around the world, representing 170 industries and 200 countries. You can find, be introduced to, and collaborate with qualified professionals.

www.business-scene.com is a regional website, which offers a great opportunity to find out what is going on with small businesses in your area.

www.xing.com has over 7 million members already use XING to manage their business contacts.

Recruitment Agencies

Recruitment is a £26.6 billion industry and has just under 1.5 million temporary workers out on assignment in any given week and places over 787,000 employees in permanent work each year. The industry sometimes has a bad reputation but it is regulated by BERR (Department for Business and Regulatory Reform). Employment agencies in England, Scotland and Wales must comply with the Employment Agencies Act 1973.

The key to finding which agency will help your job search is quite simply, to find the right one. There are thousands of national and local agencies throughout the UK and although some are generalist (they deal with anything), a large % are specialist, and concentrate on certain industries and/or skills such as:

> Industrial
> Driving
> Office Work
> I.T.
> Estate Agency
> Accountancy & Finance
> Construction
> Optical

The list goes on and on, the easiest way to find which agency you'll have the best chance of finding work with, is by checking with the REC (Recruitment and Employment Confederation), the industry's trade body.

Useful Websites

www.rec.uk.com membership is made up of over 8,000 recruitment agencies. The site has a search function to find an agency in a geographical location or by nearly 150 skill sectors.

www.agencycentral.co.uk is used by 15,000+ Employers and also has a good search engine for agencies by area, sector, and job site listings.

Below are the some of the main UK recruitment agencies:

www.reed.co.uk is also the UK's largest job site with over 100,000 jobs across all sectors by 8,000+ employers. Only a small % of jobs are actually being handled by Reed's office network as the site offers advertising for companies recruiting directly too.

www.hays.com is the largest publicly listed recruitment group in the UK and has over 8,294 staff in 380 offices across 27 countries.

www.bluearrow.co.uk is one of the UK's largest recruitment businesses, specialising in the office, industrial, catering, driving, IT and accountancy sectors.

www.adecco.co.uk has over 400 locations in England, Scotland, Wales, Northern Ireland and Ireland has more than 80 onsite alliances (offices within clients' premises). They find 250 people new permanent positions and have 35,000 temporary workers payrolled weekly.

www.manpower.co.uk employ over 30,000 people every day through a network of over 300 UK offices providing staff for around 5,000 clients.

www.brookstreet.co.uk has over 130 branches nationwide and focuses on temporary and permanent clerical, secretarial, administrative and industrial staff. They manage the recruitment needs of 15,000 clients every year.

www.hrgo.co.uk has a network of over 60 offices predominantly throughout the UK.

www.office-angels.com has over 100 branches across the country, offering secretarial, office support, administrative and call centre opportunities.

www.ranstad.co.uk is a nationwide high street branch network that operate from over 100 locations across the UK dealing with predominantly commercial/office staff on a temporary or permanent basis.

www.renfieldsearch.com has 77 offices nationwide and 15 different trading divisions.

Many agencies comply with the law, but not all of them. If you are not sure of your rights, or you want more information, you can ring the confidential Employment Agency Standards Inspectorate (EAS) Helpline 0845 955 5105.

www.campaigns.direct.gov.uk/agencyworkers also gives you online advice on your rights and how to handle complaints.

Chapter Four:

Apply...
and get noticed!

It's no good just to send applications and take a 'scatter-gun' approach. There will be an increasing number of applicants for each vacancy advertised and you need to ensure yours stands out.

Cover Letters

This is your only chance at a first impression, some employers will have made their mind up about your suitability after they have read the first one or two paragraphs of your cover letter.

Cover letters introduce your CV, they are there to persuade the reader to continue on and read your CV. They tell the reader why you want the job, why they should interview you, and that you are available. A good cover letter will show you as an excellent candidate. The CV cover letter should be written in a business format (even if you're sending your CV and cover letter via email.) This means that handwritten notes, unformatted typed or computer-generated letters are unacceptable. Recommended professional fonts are Arial or Century Gothic with a font size of 10 or 12.

Your cover letter should be concise and to the point and ideally no more than a few paragraphs.

If you can, address your letter to a person, use 'Dear Mr Jones' instead of 'Dear Mike' as it would appear too familiar. Telephone and ask the receptionist who the appropriate person is and address the letter to that person by name. If you do not know the name of the contact use 'Dear Sir or Madam'.

Your letter should include the job title along with the reference number as frequently employers are recruiting for a number of jobs.

There are three attention grabbing golden rules to writing a cover letter:

1. Remind the recruiter what they're looking for;
    "You have advertised for a property manager to manage and
    maintain your portfolio of retail outlets....."

2. Tell them you are what they're looking for -
    how you fit the job description;

    "As you will see in my attached CV, I have spent ...years
    managing a number of properties for a major retailer and have
    the ideal experience for this job."

3. Tell them why you are the best choice.

"I am very confident that I will fit perfectly into your environment and
am available for interview and can start straight away."

If you know the persons name, end your letter 'Yours sincerely', if not, end
your letter 'Yours faithfully'. Always ensure your contact details are on
your cover letter as well as on your CV.

If you apply online or enter your email address on your contact details,
think about the perception created if you have a humorous email address.
Some recruiters may not even interview you for a professional job if you
have this.

> funbobby@server.co.uk
> blondie@server.co.uk
> sicknote@server.co.uk

If you have a humorous email address – change it!

Example Cover Letter

Contact
1st Line of address
2nd Line of address
Town/City
Postcode

Date

Dear Mr Jones

Property Manager – Reference 1254/AB

I am very interested in your vacancy for a Property Manager Ref: 1254/AB which I saw advertised on/in (enter where you saw the job advertised).

You are looking for someone with previous experience of this within the retail sector whose skills are transferable and are able to make cost savings and improvements.

I have worked for a major retail group for (enter years of experience) and was responsible for making significant cost reductions throughout the supply chain. I believe my skills and experience are easily transferable and I would be the ideal candidate for this role.

I am very interested in this role, am available for interview and can start straight away.

Yours sincerely

Your name
Your address
Your contact telephone numbers

CV's

When writing your CV you should look at it through the eyes of the employer. It needs to be neat and tidy, easy to read and have all of the standard required information but most of all.... it needs to stand out from the rest.

You should tailor your CV to the job you are applying for and emphasise the skills and experience you have gained.

A CV should never be longer than two pages long as you can go into far more detail when you attend the interview.

When writing about your experience, explain how it benefited your previous employer such as improved performance, reduced costs, better efficiencies and use examples if you can.

These days, the layout and format of the CV is not important which means you can make it work for you. If your qualifications are not great, put them at the end. If you only have brief work experience but great qualifications, put them first.

What you should include:
• Introduction or Profile
• Relevant Skills
• Career/Work History
• Education and Training
• Personal Interests

Try and think about your unique selling points, what can you do or what did you do, that would make you ideal for the employer – sell yourself!

Always complete the personal interests with care, showing that you have an active personal life could be detrimental if one of your hobbies means you cannot be flexible out of hours for work commitments. Also look at it through the eyes of the recruiter, if something is perceived by most as a boring hobby that may not get you an interview for a job requiring energy and dynamism.

Never lie to try and portray a false image though, you could get caught out!

CV Template

CURRICULUM VITAE

Name: ....

Address: ....
....
....
....
....

Telephone   Home: ....
              Mobile: ....

Email Address: ....

Date of Birth: ....

Personal Profile

....
....
....
....
....
....
....
....
....
....
....

Date from - to   Name of Employer
                        Job Title
Job Description

....
....
....
....
....
....

Personal details:

Education: ....
                        ....

Date from - to   Name of School

                        Qualifications
                        ....
                        ....
                        ....
                        ....
                        ....

Professional: Memberships of Trade Bodies
                        Training Courses

Interests:

....
....
....
....
....
....

35

Applications Forms

Some employers still use application forms and more companies are making them available to download online. They do this for a number of reasons but may include ease of review if there are a large number of applications or they know where to find some specific information, such as professional qualifications, quickly and easily.

Some key guidelines are:

- Always print off a few copies first so you can practice completing them.
- Do not send application forms with errors and/or corrections on.
- If your handwriting is not great, use capitals.
- Read the instructions carefully and follow them to the letter.
- If space is limited, concentrate on areas of your experience that are most relevant.
- Use black ink.
- Get someone else to read through your practice application first, get them to be honest with you and also get them to proof read for spelling and grammar.
- Always keep a copy – and take with you to an interview.
- Never lie – you will get found out.
- Take your time.
- Do not use abbreviations, the person reading the application form may not understand them.

Many of the online job boards/sites have some very good sections on cover letters, preparing and writing CV's.

Useful Websites
www.monster.co.uk
www.jobsite.co.uk
www.totaljobs.co.uk
www.reed.co.uk
www.fish4.co.uk

Chapter Five:
Your Big Chance - The Interview

You've done the hard-work getting yourself an interview in todays climate, so make it count! This is your chance, you need to be prepared and focused.

Company Research

A common complaint by interviewers is that when asking a candidate what they know about their company, they know nothing. The more you know, the better, not only to appear knowledgeable and interested but also to make sure it's the kind of company you want to work for.

• Check the company's website and read every page.
• If they are a PLC (Public Limited Company), they will prepare an Annual Report. This will tell you about the company, its structure, financials and their locations amongst other things.
• If the interview is through an agency, your consultant can give you more information.
• Phone the Head Office and ask the receptionist to post you a corporate brochure.

Useful Website

www.londonstockexchange.ar.wilink.com Free information on the performance and intentions of over 1,300 listed companies, no research tool is more valuable than a company's annual report.

Getting There

It is completely unacceptable to arrive late for an interview. If you are late, for whatever reason, you are already looked at in a poor light. Plan your route and aim to get to the location about 10-15 minutes early and don't rely on sat-nav.

Useful Websites

www.traveline.org.uk The UK's No 1 website for impartial information on planning your journey, by bus, coach or train... or any combination of the three.

www.multimap.com In association with the RAC, this site has maps, route planners and travel times.

First Impressions

The famous saying is true, you have one chance. Wear smart business attire, regardless of the kind of job you're applying for. When you are sitting in the waiting area/reception, sit up straight, look confident and make sure your mobile phone is switched off!

When you are greeted by the interviewer, maintain good eye contact (without glaring) and give them a firm handshake. Don't try to break their hand and if you get sweaty palms, make sure you have a handkerchief in your pocket. The interviewer will certainly remember you if you crush his hand or have a limp, damp handshake – but not in a good way. Practice on your friends/family and ask their opinion.

Wait until you're offered a chair before you sit down, you wouldn't want to sit at the wrong desk!

Finally, go alone – don't take children or friends, it's you they are interviewing.

Question & Answer Techniques

Your interview will go a lot smoother if you have prepared enough and how you answer the questions is crucial. Think about what kind of questions will be asked, some general and some specific to the role and have the answers ready, here are some of the most common:

- Tell me about yourself.
  (This is often an ice-breaker question. Keep the answer job or skill related.)
- What do you know about the type of work we do?
  (This is your chance to tell them what you know from the research you completed ahead of time.)
- Why do you want to work here?
  (Keep it job or company related and positive)

- What is your weakness?
  (Always make this a positive answer. For example, "My spelling is not always perfect, so I always use a spell checker.")
- What are your strengths?
  (Describe your skills in a way that will show you as a desirable employee for the company.)
- Why did you leave your last job?
  (Answer with a positive statement - "new job," "contract ended," "seasonal," "temporary," "career change," "returned to school," "to raise a family," or "relocated.")
- Why have you been unemployed for such a long time?
  (Tell the truth. Emphasize that you were looking for a good company where you can settle and make a contribution.)
- Why should we employ you?
  (Make a positive statement, such as "I would like the opportunity to work with you and believe that I can make a valuable contribution to your company.")
- Where do you see yourself in five years?
  (Obviously with the same employer but tailor your answer to the job and company. Not all interviewers are looking for dynamism and money motivated career people, they may just want stability!)

Your Questions

Once you have answered all of their questions, they will usually ask you if you have any. This is an opportunity to show that you are keen to get the job and want to do it well.

Here are some examples:

- What will be my responsibilities?
- Where will I fit into the overall organisational structure?
- Who will I report to?
- Where does he/she fit in the structure?
- Who will report to me?
- How experienced are they?
- What is expected of me in the first 6 months?

- What level of performance do you expect from me?
- Who are your customers?
- Where is the company going? Upwards? Expansion plans?
- What are the chances of advancement/promotion in this position?
- What will be my salary, benefits and bonuses?
  (Do not bring this up too early in the interview - wait until they are sold on you.)
- Will travelling be required in this position?
- Will relocation be required now or in the future?
- What training do you provide?
- When will you decide on the appointment?
- What is the next step?

You will notice that all of these questions started with who, what, where and when. These are called open questions and are designed so that the person answering the question has to give more information. Questions other than these are called closed questions and usually their answer will be a straight yes or no!

Presentations

It's not unusual when recruiting for senior roles, or where presentations are going to be part of the job, to ask candidates to make a presentation as part of their interview. This is an excellent opportunity to show your potential employers what you can do, away from the formal interview question and answers procedure.

Preparing your presentation

The most important thing is to know who you're going to be speaking to. This will inevitably influence what you say and how you pitch your presentation. Find out how many people will be on the panel, their status, their expertise, any knowledge levels you can safely assume, and whether they know each other.

Once you've established these details, you can get to work on the all-important structure.

Getting the right structure

You should always have one clear message that runs through your presentation, and limit yourself to three sections: introduction, development of your argument and summary. Any more than that and your presentation will lose focus.

Develop a powerful introduction and close, as these are the times when your audience will be most attentive. Ensure that your ideas are clear and come in a logical sequence, using sentences that are short and to the point. When calculating how much time to devote to each section, allow 10-15% for your opening, the same for your conclusion, and the rest for the main content.

A clear delivery

Keep your opening punchy and have a memorable ending that will leave your audience on an upbeat note. Speak slowly and with purpose; avoid rambling or making digressions. Make regular eye contact with members of your audience, rather than allowing your gaze to drift vaguely round the room or over their heads.

Try to learn your presentation by heart. It will save you having to fumble around with prompt cards or PowerPoint slides and will give an excellent impression of your confidence and professionalism. However you choose to present, practice your presentation beforehand, testing it on friends or family if you have the chance.

If you are giving handouts of the presentation alway take a spare copy.

Taking questions

Dealing with questions gives you the opportunity to further demonstrate your knowledge of your subject. Let your audience know in advance that you will be willing to take questions at the end so they don't disrupt the flow of you presentation.

Take your time to answer, be ready to defend yourself and don't argue with a questioner. If you do come up against a conflict of opinions, don't try to win the battle - search for a good compromise position. Inviting other questions or views from the other members of the audience may help you diffuse a potentially prickly situation.

Finally, enjoy it. It's a great chance to shine!

Telephone Interviews

Companies often prefer to conduct telephone (screening) interviews before inviting candidates to their offices for a face-to-face interview.

This applies particularly:

• When candidates will have to travel a long way
• When there are large numbers of candidates
• When screening by CV is difficult
 (when for example, personality is more important than experience or qualification)
• When a large part of the job will involve talking to people on the telephone.

A telephone interview should be treated in the same way as a normal interview and should be taken as seriously. The person you speak to will have a series of questions that they will want to ask you and will certainly want to elaborate on your CV.

Before you are scheduled in to conduct the interview, jot down all the answers to the most commonly asked questions and have that in front of you so you can then refer to these. Try however, to answer them in a natural way.

Here are some tips:
- Have a notepad, pen and diary handy.
- Have your CV at hand. Prepare mentally, or better still in writing to answer the 'Tell me about yourself' question.
- If you have been asked to call at a specific time, call at the correct time. Too early shows over-keenness and may damage your negotiating position later on, or your chances of getting to the next stage. Too late shows lack of interest - excuses won't be tolerated. If you can't get through (manager busy), leave a message with the secretary/receptionist to show that you called at the right time.
- Think about how you normally answer the phone at home. When you answer the phone, do so by announcing your name, in an enthusiastic style: 'John Pickles, Good Morning!' If this is not your natural style, change it!
- Sound interesting/interested, energetic and enthusiastic
- Don't waffle.
- Don't use jargon
- Don't swear
- Be polite
- Don't use your mobile phone unless you have to. Mobile phones rarely allow your voice to sound as clear as a standard land line and you risk losing the signal.
- Be courteous and try not to speak over the interviewer or cut them off. If you do, apologise and let the interviewer continue.
- Do not hang up until the interviewer has hung up.
- Stand up – research shows that you sound more confident and assertive if you do.

Positive Attitude

- Show enthusiasm for the job in your tone of voice, the things you say, and your body language.

- Focus on the positive things. Just as with your written application, avoid negative words and phrases like 'limited', 'only', 'very little', 'I don't have ....', 'All I did was .....' etc.

- Focus on what you can do instead. You need to be honest with the panel, but instead of saying something like 'No, I haven't used Microsoft Excel', talk about relevant things you have done, e.g. 'I haven't used Microsoft Excel, but I have used a number of other spreadsheet packages, including ....'

- If you have things to say about yourself that you think are particularly relevant to the job and you haven't been asked them, you can raise these at the end of the interview.

It could be about issues which haven't been discussed but which you think are particularly important to the job, e.g. initiative, working well in a team, etc. Alternatively, you may want to mention personal strengths which you think are important to the job, e.g. conscientiousness, loyalty, adaptability, etc.

Close the Deal

You have got over the various hurdles and have managed to get this far on the skills you have gained. Now is your big chance, the interviewer may be impressed but you have to convince them that not only is your experience and personality what he is looking for, but he doesn't need to look at anyone else and therefore should offer you a job!

Closing Questions

When the interview comes to a close, the interviewer will usually ask you if there is anything else you would like to know and/or add, here are some killer questions:

- What reservations do you have about offering me the job? This brings out any concerns they have about you i.e.: "you do live quite a distance from the office" can easily be countered with "I have travelled the same distance to work for the last ten years, so I can definitely say travelling is not a problem."
- Ask for the Job! Recap your strengths and suitability for the job and that you're very interested and ask "what is the next step?"

If the interviewer is still not committing enough, offer a 'free work trial', this is where you offer to work for free for one-two days. It gives the interviewer a couple of things 1) the opportunity to try you out 2) show them how committed and keen you are.

Rejections
The reality is that you may get rejected for jobs you apply for. The key is to learn from any rejections and be persistent. You may have been in a job for a number of years and this was your first interview for some time, of course you will be rusty. With each interview attended, you'll feel more confident, less nervous and handle any questions or concerns raised in a far better way.

- Analyse your interview and try to find where you may have gone wrong to improve for next time.
- Don't get angry, defensive or despondent – it will come across in future interviews.
- Don't argue the point – it's rare they will change their mind.
- Remain positive.

Above all – don't give up,
be persistent,
stay focused and you will...

Index

www.ingramcontent.com/pod-product-compliance
Lightning Source LLC
Chambersburg PA
CBHW021931170526
45157CB00005B/2270